With You There
and Me Here

With You There and Me Here

Edited by Susan Polis Schutz
Designed and Illustrated by Stephen Schutz

in conjunction with SandPiper Studios

Blue Mountain Press ™

Boulder, Colorado

Library of Congress Number: 78-73395
ISBN: 0-88396-041-9

Manufactured in the United States of America

Special thanks to Lucy Hackett, Douglas Pagels, Richard Schoenberger
and Sarah Jones.

First Printing: January, 1979
Second Printing: May, 1979
Third Printing: October, 1980

ACKNOWLEDGMENTS are on page 64.

Blue Mountain Press INC.

P.O. Box 4549, Boulder, Colorado 80306

CONTENTS

With you there
and me here
I have had no one
to discuss little things with
like how the dew feels on the grass
or big things like
what's going on in the world

I have been lonely
talking and thinking to myself
I now realize how essential it is
to have someone
to share oneself with

Susan Polis Schutz

Friends are not only
together when they
are side-by-side,
even one who is far away . . .
is still in our thoughts.

Ludwig van Beethoven

I know how alone you are
. . . it's so hard
to be so far
from the ones
who mean the most to you
when you would
so much rather
have them close . . .
you know
my love is always there

Carole King

I want for you
what you want
for yourself.
I want to be near you,
but the only
essential nearness
is the nearness
of understanding.
I want to be with you,
in will and desire.

I love you.

Mary Haskell

Thinking of home
Thinking of the past
Thinking of tomorrow
Brings me closer to you
You are a special person
who brings lasting joy
into my life

Louise Bradford Lowell

*Roses and moonlight
dancing on air
don't mean a thing
if you're not there*

*walking beside me
living inside me*

Hoyt Axton

We were so close to each other that I hardly feel even yet as if we are really separated. I am with you in spirit constantly.

Ellen Wilson

I am only half myself away from you . . . I can't be altogether miserable in your absence because I know that it is only absence of body — that the heart that makes my life so bright and happy — which is my life's self — is with me . . .

Woodrow Wilson

I know what my heart wants of you . . .
to lie close to you
and let the world rush by.
To watch with you
suns rising and moons rising . . .
to hear high music
that only birds can hear.

Edna St. Vincent Millay

*There are sweet smiles here,
and I shall hear some singing . . .
I always do when I leave
any place or person
that is specially beautiful.*

*When I am in the midst
of the greatest beauty,
I remind myself that it is so,
but I do not seem
to touch the very heart;
but when I have left it behind
then its heart overflows itself
in the remembrance,
and so the past
becomes more beautiful
than any possible present.*

George William Curtis

A friend so rare
you stand by me no matter what
the good or bad of my life
you never disappoint me
when i need to depend on your support . . .
you tell me when i am wrong
so gently you guide me without pain
you love me even when we disagree
each day and night i feel your presence
you may not be near to touch
but you are in my mind and heart
you meet my needs so silently
i am not alone because of you
whatever i am that causes you
to love me with this loyalty . . . i pray
that i am as much for you
as you are for me
my friend i love you

Diane Westlake

*The sight of a written word
from you would be
the next best thing
to the sight
of your face
or the touch
of your hand.*

Algernon Charles Swinburne

Today is very beautiful —
just as bright,
just as blue,
just as green and as white
and as crimson
as the cherry trees
in full bloom,
and the half-opening peach blossoms
and the grass just waving,
and sky and hill and cloud
can make it,
if they try.

How I wish
you were here.

Emily Dickinson

You give me space
to belong to myself
yet without separating me
from your own life.
May it all turn out
to your happiness.

Johann Wolfgang von Goethe

*E*very day I live
I discover
more and more
how impossible it is
for me
to live without you.

James Hackman

You leave
your memory
as a flame
to my lonely lamp
of separation.

Rabindranath Tagore

Miss you, miss you, miss you;
Everything I do
Echoes with the laughter
And the voice of you
You're on every corner,
Every turn and twist,
Every old familiar spot
Whispers how you're missed.

Miss you, miss you, miss you.
Everywhere I go
There are poignant memories
Dancing in a row,

Silhouette and shadow
Of your form and face
Substance and reality
Everywhere displace.

Oh, I miss you, miss you . . .
There's a strange, sad silence
'Mid the busy whirl,
Just as tho' the ordinary,
Daily things I do
Wait with me, expectant,
For a word from you . . .

David Cory

I do not want to make reasons
for you
to stay,
Only reasons
for you
to return.

jonivan

The world is so empty
if one thinks only of
mountains, rivers and cities;
but to know someone who
thinks and feels with us,
and who, though distant,
is close to us in spirit,
this makes the earth
for us an inhabited garden.

Johann Wolfgang von Goethe

*Thank you for all the kindness
I have received from you,
and for all the affection
you have shown me,
throughout the course of my years:
the only return I can make
is by gratitude
the deepest and most enduring:
and love the most devoted:
and although removed by fortune
to a distance from you,
my heart is always with you . . .*

Ellen Randolph Coolidge

I *feel that we should*
both be happy,
if we could
be together.

Walt Whitman

I **keep thinking
about you
every few minutes
all day.**

Walt Whitman

i carry your heart with me(i carry it in
my heart)i am never without it(anywhere
i go you go,my dear;and whatever is done
by only me is your doing,my darling)

                                    i fear
no fate(for you are my fate,my sweet)i want
no world(for beautiful you are my world,my true)
and it's you are whatever a moon has always meant
and whatever a sun will always sing is you

here is the deepest secret nobody knows
(here is the root of the root and the bud of the bud
and the sky of the sky of a tree called life;which grows
higher than soul can hope or mind can hide)
and this is the wonder that's keeping the stars apart

i carry your heart(i carry it in my heart)

        e.e. cummings

I always imagine
that if I were near you now,
I should profit more by
the gift of your presence —
just as one feels
about all past sunlight.

George Eliot

We are . . . affectionate in our memories of our too far-off friend. I often see you enjoying your sunsets and the wayside flowers.

George Eliot

I and my heart
put ourselves in your hands,
begging you to recommend us
to your good grace
and not to let absence
lessen your affection . . .
for although by absence
we are parted,
it nevertheless
keeps its fervency.

King Henry VIII

Love reckons
hours for months
and days
for years;

And every little absence
is an age.

John Dryden

*Love, the magician,
knows this little trick
whereby two people walk
in different directions
yet always remain
side by side.*

Hugh Prather

May the memory
of my love
follow and comfort you
during our separation.
If you only knew how much
I love you,
how essential you are
to my life,
you would not dare
to stay away for an instant,
you would always remain
by my side,
your heart pressed
close to my heart,
your soul
to my soul.

Juliette Drouet

If it is true, as you told me,
that you are all the time thinking of me,
it is one of my greatest happinesses
to believe that this sweet,
intimate correspondence of thought
continually brings our souls together,
even when we are not near each other.

Victor Hugo

You and I

We ought to be together — you and I;

We want each other so, to comprehend
The dream, the hope, things planned,
   or seen, or wrought.

Companion, comforter and guide
   and friend,
As much as love asks love,
   does thought ask thought.

Life is so short, so fast
   the lone hours fly,

We ought to be together, you and I.

Henry Alford

*When the ways
of friends
converge,
the whole world
looks like home.*

Hermann Hesse

I don't like to feel anything in between us;
Not one dang thing in between us;
All these ways and distances
And miles and trials and bottles and vials and
Hammers and files
From where I'm here at
To where you're now atting'
Betwixt and between us;
From me to you there;
Or from you over to me here;
From
You to me.

Woody Guthrie

Remember me,
as I do you,
with all the tenderness
which it is possible for one
to feel for another,
which no time can obliterate,
no distance alter,
but which is always the same.

Abigail Adams

Because there was a seed
A pine has grown even here
On these barren rocks:
If we really love our love
What can keep us from meeting?

Anonymous

Far from you
there is no joy;
far from you,
the world is a desert
where I live alone
without experiencing
the sweetness of opening out my heart.
You have taken from me
more than my soul;
you are the one thought
of my life.

Napoleon

God bless and protect you,
and give you strength and courage
and grant that we may soon meet
to part no more,
but to live to comfort each other
for the future
in peace and tranquility.

C.J. Mathews

*Two lovers
should never be
so far apart
that they cannot
bring each other
a rose
still fresh
and blooming.*

Nikolaus Lenau

I wish heartily
we were together somewhere,
for I want you,
selfishly want you, often;
and the glimpses I get
at you through letters,
is something like what we have
of the sun at this season —
very bright, but distant . . .

Thomas Moore

Today I have been happy.
All the day I held memory of you,
and wove its laughter
with the dancing light of the spray,
and sowed the sky
with tiny clouds of love,
and sent you following
the white waves of sea . . .

Rupert Brooke

*You know that
however much time
passes without you
hearing from me,
there is not a day
that does not in some way . . .
bring me nearer to you
or remind me
of your friendship . . .
and your life.*

Felix Mendelssohn

If you knew the power
of a word, a look, a kind expression,
or a caress from you,
and from what distant countries
one of these could bring me,
you would be convinced . . .
that nothing is equal
to your presence!

Madame De Sevigne

You went away,
leaving me with
the memories we made
Memories of those
sweet yesterdays
spent with you

And even though
you're gone,
I still think
so often
of you

Dolly Parton

I wish you good spaces
in the far away places
you go.

If it rains or it snows,
may you be safe and warm . . .

And if you need somebody
sometime, you know I will
always be there.

Gordon Lightfoot

We may have
been apart
but the ties
between us
have gotten closer
The memory of the
times we have spent together
shall last forever

Louise Bradford Lowell

Sweet is
  The sunbreak
  After the rain

Welcome is
  The breeze
  That follows the heat

Warm is
  The fire
  Against the snow

Yet none
  So precious
  As your smile
  That says

    Welcome home . . .

After we've
  Been apart

Leonard Nimoy

ACKNOWLEDGMENTS

Alfred A. Knopf for "I want you," by Mary Haskell. From the book BELOVED PROPHET: The Love Letters of Kahlil Gibran and Mary Haskell, and Her Private Journal, by Kahlil Gibran and Mary Haskell, edited and arranged by Virginia Hilu. Copyright © 1972 by Alfred A. Knopf, Inc. All rights reserved. Reprinted by permission of the publisher.

Diane Westlake for "A friend so rare," by Diane Westlake. From the book GENTLE FREEDOM, Copyright © 1977 Diane Westlake. Published by Honor Press. All rights reserved. Reprinted by permission.

Doubleday & Company, Inc. for "Love, the magician," by Hugh Prather. From the book NOTES ON LOVE AND COURAGE. Copyright © 1977 by Hugh Prather. All rights reserved. Used by permission.

Harcourt Brace Jovanovich, Inc. for "i carry your heart with me," by e. e. cummings. From the book COMPLETE POEMS 1913-1962. Copyright © 1952 by E. E. Cummings. All rights reserved. Reprinted by permission.

Harold Ober Associates Incorporated for "We were so close," by Ellen Wilson. And for "I am only," by Woodrow Wilson. From the book THE PRICELESS GIFT, published by Alfred A. Knopf, Inc. Copyright © 1962 by Eleanor Wilson McAdoo. All rights reserved. Reprinted by permission.

Harper & Brothers for "I know what my heart," by Edna St. Vincent Millay. From the book LETTERS OF EDNA ST. VINCENT MILLAY, edited by Allan Ross Macdougall. Published by Harper & Brothers. © Copyright 1952 by Norma Millay Ellis. © Copyright 1952 by Allan Ross Macdougal. All rights reserved. Reprinted by permission.

Hoyt Axton for "Roses and moonlight," by Hoyt Axton. From the song ROSES AND MOONLIGHT. Copyright © 1970, 1972 Lady Jane Music. International Copyright Secured. All rights reserved. Reprinted by permission.

jonivan for "I do not want," by jonivan. From the book THE THOUGHT WELL, Copyright © jonivan, 1975. All rights reserved. Reprinted by permission.

Leonard Nimoy for "Sweet is the sunbreak," by Leonard Nimoy. From the book COME BE WITH ME, published by Blue Mountain Press, Inc. Copyright © Leonard Nimoy, 1978. All rights reserved. Reprinted by permission.

Macmillan Publishing Co., Inc. for "I don't like," by Woody Guthrie. From the book BORN TO WIN, edited by Robert Shelton. Copyright © The Guthrie Children's Trust Fund 1965. All rights reserved. Reprinted by permission.

Owepar Publishing Co. for "You went away," by Dolly Parton. From the song WE USED TO. Copyright © 1975 by Owepar Publishing Co. All rights reserved. Used by permission.

Screen Gems-EMI Music, Inc. and Colgems-EMI Music, Inc. for "I know how alone," by Carole King. From the song GOODBYE DON'T MEAN I'M GONE. Copyright © 1972 Colgems Music Corp. All rights reserved. Reprinted by permission.

Warner Bros., Inc. for "I wish you good spaces," by Gordon Lightfoot. From the song I'M NOT SUPPOSED TO CARE. Copyright © 1976 Moose Music Ltd. All rights reserved. Reprinted by permission.

A careful effort has been made to trace the ownership of poems used in this anthology in order to get permission to reprint copyrighted poems and to give proper credit to the copyright owners.

If any error or omission has occurred, it is completely inadvertent, and we would like to correct it in future editions provided that written notification is made to the publisher: BLUE MOUNTAIN PRESS, INC., P.O. Box 4549, Boulder, Colorado 80306